As the Toad Sleeps

By Ferris E. Jones

Copyright 2007
By Ferris E. Jones
All rights reserved

ISBN : 978-0-6151-7714-4
ID:1395906
www.lulu.com

This book is dedicated in loving memory to my sister Dodie. I would like to thank my wife Tina for her support, and my mother Kathy for all her hard work.

Sister at the Gates

Each day of times consumption
hands thrust together in prayer.
to speak a whisper for the souls
who still walk the sadden step,
and give distinction to those who have
 passed through the gambol gates.

This day is for the sister
 and her name moves the order.
 She had traversed this stride
 with the days watery passing,
 to hold the door open
 until a loved ones name is silently spoken.

The Beats

If the beats are all gone
who will tell the stories
of Mongoloid children attacking
strangers with shovels? Not
knowing why it is wrong.
Plays will not be written
from their dreams,
actors will never play the
teenage boys raping
the neighbor girl. Then
display her nipples as a prize
like a little boy's hot wheel.
Someone needs to tell
the yarns of the autistic,
with the flare of the SLA
in the burning house.

Clapton

When the story was told he was three
the ground lined hot with tar.
The open window hung as a gateway
for the ghosts praying to be saved.

Traveling, waiting for the moment that
God fingers the way to redemption.

With a push out of God's favor the
child's face becomes hot with the pain
and a man's destiny is foredoomed.

For circling like light buzzards are angels
fighting for their place to be anywhere
than with those who failed with God's son.

Lucy's Diamond was Stolen

   Sitting in church smug with the
    arrogance of a Bishop unrestrained.
   The man; articulates that no applause
  be allowed this day. Only the Lord's
picture will leave an imprint
from within these walls.
The president has been taken
to the hospital so contact our many
investments and declare all viewing
must be stopped at once. From these walls
he does decree.

Knight of the Round Disease

Amount; type of unforeseen vengeance
coming from a hair-lipped virgin
whose crying brings forth such a
roar as to move the Pope's home
to Israel. Giving back that which was
once bloody with the souls of
dead feet walking on the
skins of lizards and snakes. Slipping
closer each day to the treaty
of contempt; which will someday
bring back the war which can
be seen from the heavens.
For it is an angel's prize to
kidnap the young and make them
the knights of the round disease.

Raven Juice

Deep fried snake spit serves
him well as the ringleader.
His gray ghost will
equal a dead Kennedy.

Forget the threat of desert
death not seen
by children who play games
of daily Raman noodles.

So drink this raven juice
and call upon your friends
to help serve the daughters
the reek of political virginity.

Collage of Souls

Everyday as the water runs down
    I ask God
    to bless those
    that ask for rest
    peace
    for the one's who are gone.
    They appear
    as a thought;
    a collage of souls
    like a picture
    on a white wall.
    All the faces
    I hope to see,
    their happy
    rested
    they look after the children
    guide our steps
    and make our marks.

I know Where the Knife Went

I know where the knife went,
the palm print, blood unanswered
painted a trail back
to everybody wondering loosely drunk
never to speak of this judgment.

The dark brown loss of encouragement
puddles changes as if life exhaled
the parking lots capture. Like another
whore's wisdom resting on the words
displayed on a bar nap.

It was simple, how chaos chose this
venue for its recourse.
The gangster words were written to
be read by peasants overlooking
the canyon of an open chest.

My Grandfather

I left the bones
in the closet,
in a burlap bag.
Did anyone ever find them?
Did they call the police?
Bury the bones, say nothing,
keep them?
There was once the thought,
that these were the bones
of my grandfather.
I would sit on the floor
trying to put the bones together
maybe he could be back.
I never could make it work
something was missing
I didn't know where it went.
Even now without the bones
I can't piece it together
and still I wonder what
happened to that bag of bones,
   my Grandfather.

A Poet in the Rain

We are the beat
not traveled, wasted on the
fast food spit
out at us.
Like the rain which
covers our fine words.
We stand
aware of not being
fraid of big brother,
or the people who
ask for the tears
not found when speaking
of a word that
    never sees the page.

Seeing

The spirits with blood crying
to be seen
cannot dream.
As they pour the hallways and
visions for children. They
ask for a good next day.

In the winter they chop
wood to heat the dreams.
Then look into the faces
of those they have lost.
Seeing what is true
lies in the children.

Those who travel with the light, on
the balls of their feet, will leave
the dreams and visions for the children.

The Map

Look at the cartography ,
boundaries change as the water flows
troops to help an endless Zion.
Thousands of beasts come forward
to eat the meat of the dying.

It must be bearded fame with license
to father a day with a CNN whore.
That declares war against Christendom.
But the day will rise again and
a great monkey will rule all the animals.

Myself

I'm trying to send myself back
to revolt from leaving the warm
water which was my beginning.

But the tedious moments of
transgressions have formed a barrier
which this Trojan horse cannot steer.

No matter what my fate; that it be
the death of nonsense trickling
down the walls of an Aztec city.

Or the surrender of this life to
another who declares me unfit
will I ever refuse to be myself.

A Plane over a Burning Forest

Adopted parts of broken homes can
carry a child a Zodiac away.
Just as drunken laughter befalls
the trees in a burning forest.

Animals must run blind
in a world where homes are only
holes, transferable like Christ,
who gave stars for competition. There
was a malfunction when it came to
the number of the virgins. So the
lizard king was forced
to go hide in Africa
                    with the first man.

The Darkness

Cry not for thy soul
nor for thy pity.
In containment the journeys
travel obscures any such
notion those evenings drenched
with holes will ever be filled.
The answers will always be safe.

It is in the darkness
that forced imagination becomes
a trite cycle concluding
in the behest
of words
swimming
to an island world
where the faithful drown
the fools behave
and every one has a bong.

The Flame

The flame played on long after
the time zone eyed Wisconsin.
It was the right thing to do
not taking it was
the only thing that matters
now for the young wicked girl.
Victory for a drunken pirate
who simply boards
another ship
loaded with rum
headed fast
into the wind
slowly pillaging
      of his own life.

Crumbling Bricks

In error are humans
    eclipsed by which
    there is nothing.
Spending the day away
    with memories of
the crumbling bricks
    not knowing why
messages are engraved.
With slow written books
    and wine as ink
we will dine on the fruits
    of discontent
then smile our way away.

A Mother's Servant

Its work,
the precarious knowledge which
one uses to chastise.
Talking in jabs out-loud
to astonish
the medley for the elongated
route. With obsessed arguments
of a knotted lament it always
goes past
the camouflage of its end.
As mothers servants
scream it's not my fault.

Divorce

A blade of grass, dried
lays outstretched; alone
on top of a bed
without corners, trying to cool.
The comfort of a hand
 is distant
 in its years of growth.
The sun goes down begging
showing as
early as it can.
The grass thirsts
 for the missing food
             in the sunshine.

Door Bell

Always knowing where the clover
with four sides hides, only
accentuates the unbearable
nature from which life sets
its designs for man.

To be part of the unmistakable
house; without closing a door
bringing about a why should we
crawl or kneel in search of an
icon seen only in one's head?

Bending down to pick up such
an item only reminds us of the
age closer to death which
rings its door bell; never
to be heard in an empty house.

They Walk Everywhere

They are here, everywhere
but we cannot see them.
To be; does not mean
right here
 where you are
 in one spot.
Cities of them pass in us
giving us the day
to live through.
They speak to each other,
sometimes we hear them.
The crazy man on the
corner fears them not.
Some say
more than one leader
comes from these cities
to tell of death
to some people
        as they sleep.

The Virgin

Even after all these years
she reminds me
of not knowing God.
But I have met him,
he lives here
with me.
I brought him out
to show her once.
Here he is
three feet tall
red hair
blue eyes
and freckles.
 I'm sure it's him
 I saw the creation
 I watched him
 just appear.
Was he there with you?
You're divorced?
Did you see him,
when you had sex?

Ball and Chain

   Forgetting for a time
the night terrors
the ball and chain floats
on sunny days.

It's the rain at
two o'clock
in a car sleeping with
nothing on the no walls
nothing on the no bed
no parents again
when the floating begins
to deliver.
Setting up for
the late night scream.

Dead

Those who beg
      cry.
Those who beg
      die.
Those who beg
respond carelessly to God.
Those who beg
drink alcohol, smell their pants,
fall prey to smaller animals.
Those who beg
eat fruit and nuts
fallen from years ago.
Those who beg
should be like Ginsberg
and remain quiet.

Cheap Beer and Cigarettes

A very old parking lot
scattered with cars,
some homes.
Cheap beer and cigarettes
light the entrance
to family shopping.
Only three carts
one
two blocks away.
Kids with stolen bikes
make go carts
with the wheels.
The bar next door
has specials
for all dads.
The nights shadow falls
on an oil stained side walk.

Drunk Driver

Wyatt Earp, in his travels
in a fog sees
a body lying there.
  It wasn't a gun shot, but
it was still a body
  with a hole in the heart.
No more time to see
  just brown lying around,
   and the faces looking down.
Bloody people dazed
nobody did it,
they were all innocent.
  The Vietnam vet sitting
   talking about the blood
the stains
the things he saw
the things he did.
  They were all innocent.
Yet somehow
there was a dead man
in a parking lot
  with a hole in his heart,
all because someone
didn't want to
drive drunk.

Oh So Important

Drunken speech,
the written word
was oh so important
when laced with pious contempt.

The yellow fingers holding the pen
gleamed bright with the flickering
of hypnotic thought.

Then with the ego of the pharaohs
and the light growing in secret,
we have all worlds of the divine.

The pyramid of the prophecy
sees a night of religion,
only to be lost somewhere
in the Bucket of Blood Saloon.

Watching

Watching young people
roping cattle; I don't
know why it made me smile.
It must be the sun
shining over the brown
mountains hiding the dirt
bikes noise happily.
Or the posts of all
different sizes
 roping wire along the
field of rabbit food.
Most of the time they
would shoot at them,
   but not this day.

Prostitution and Kennedy

Looking forward and moving down
a river flows with the
electrical power it provides.
A house of business lies in
the shade of the mountain
serving cocktails of the soul
between the pages of an unread Bible.
It is legal; or sanctioned
 by the Irish church which is separate
from the state which allows God
to walk through the open door;
in an attempt to create
values the news can use to
explain the killing of an American.

Letters

My only time
my only mind
is now in my hands.
I cannot see the people;
forgot how I got here.

I hear there are words,
they translate into
only passing letters
never read them.

Light is of great importance
to the mind
up or down
many letters
fly past
 Dorothy's house.

The Grey's

All dressed up in
his finest abstinence
he struts the streets
in search of the wares
hidden from a past response.
Declaring the untold truth
with each swagger
that God has forsaken
the meaning of his being,
and mute to his height
in a society of gray's.
His hands hold his head
high above all the others as
he passes on his journey.

Learned vs. Innate

Nobody can control the rage:
it's a sentence imposed by birth,
   discontented Karma
   has been actualized
   in this experiment.

   A cage with no bars
   with roads only
   west
   the door is open
   to a reward.

   High liquid
   reaching
   for travel not enough
   to fear
   mother and father.

7-11

The streets are clean,
the birds saunter without burden.
Sounds of summer escape
with a splash and crack.
In shelters, sustenance
is real and music
from the all star game explodes.
Boys are packed on bikes
to conquer 7-11
to get that coke slurpee
and its spoon.
All to just sit
and watch the game
while the ice turns white.

What if God

What if God
played over and over
with a hundred dollar bill?
Making it appear out of reach,
maybe the ink runs.
Floating it upwards as
a song continues to play.
With ears ringing
and people around
in an almost circle
it floats again.
Then the morning paper;
Capricorns can
speak to the divine,
get closer to God,
see him, feel him,
talk directly to him,
and get answers from him.
If they follow the
money trail.

Gates

If the gates of heaven were opened
   to all for just one day.
   Who would be seen in a glow
   without a flame?
   Would Martin Luther King be
   seated next to Thomas Jefferson
   while a Confederate flag hangs
   high waving?

And if the gates of hell were opened
   to all for just one day.
   Who would be seen in the
   pit of fire without a light?
   Would Adolph Hitler be
   seated next to Nostradamus
   while his staff stands stiff
               in the water?

The News

On what day will a
mother's eye tear
to walk
the path of dread,
the bloody thorns
pushed on and around
the head of the unbeliever.

When will a distance
be shown
cracking, laughing,
burning with the sun
destruction of greenery
and a dog unheard.

You #1

I'm the man who places
that small curtain
above your window.
The one who obscures
your vision,
only in part.
I can stop the sun
from coming
upon your face.
Without ever asking you
for anything.
I'm the one you wish
to kick,
when the blanket
covers your feet,
and the one
you seek to hold
when the snow
is falling deep.

Evolution

What evolution has brought us here?
Where winged creatures fly so fiercely
with deliberate species calculation.
What age has dissolved the upward pleasure?
To burrow and hoard amongst the
very vastness of fossils, clinging
to the dirt from which it crawled.
Is it to be the wings?
Unfortunate begetting of brethren with
claws that must fight, always
for survival emerging from the caves

Word

The eclipse was
last night.
But its echo
still lingers.
Over the trees
the clouds paint
like morning rain.
A speck of blue brings
drops to the heart
and pain
upon a word,
so hard it
is to be spoken
everyday.

Smooth

The smooth polished hardness
sits quietly in a child's hand
cascading vast crevices.

The beauty withstood the outspoken
motive of energy leading to its
birth between land and sea.

Placed just from a time
as a dust to blow back
to its home
    between land and sea.

Noah's Ark

Many eyes witnessed
the loading of the ark.
Couples or pairs
all creatures were placed,
next to those who had
never seen such wonders.
A black man and woman
lay together with the Jew
who cried when the King
sat with his mistress
and the cat,
  as the toad sleeps.

The Girl in White

No mark has secured this
bridge rarely traveled.
The shortness of white
portrays the years as
painted with trouble.

It disturbs a beginning,
the adolescent atrocities
in disguise,
a foreboding
detail accessed,
spindling of thoughts
born inside of depths.

John the English

The modern papacy was not
defined by ancient scripture,
but re-written as a new
type of book in twelve languages.
It contains the views of
women like John the English
giving birth to a child.
Always uncovering a lie,
not being that which God
has put forth.
Takes a piece away
from the form
        of belief.

A Coffee Can in the Attic

It's folded over by machines
holding the DNA of mankind.
With blood, objects are placed inside
delicately, hiding it for a time.

Shells sound the children's walk
playing wet with earth clinging.
A distant memory presses
against the heads of the forgotten.

A skull, dead like Nevada cattle,
a Texas tie gets placed inside
to be gone until life gets
remodeled or
children rule the present.

Naked

The pure naked coin
was not enough to stop the
crucifixion of our son.
The balance of money and power
would never be passed over,
from that moment forward.
Those who are to work
for that band of gold displayed
on the sleeve of indulgence,
go home to have supper only
when the phone stops ringing.

College

The leaves are what are remembered,
laughing in it's gathering of corners.
The sun sleeps its short day
and the dread of pain sets a lovely table
for the one who stays behind.

The dreams are held by writing in moods
to the music of long phone calls.
Praising them each night to sleep,
in the silence of what was once
a necklace of laughter.

The thoughts are believed to be
centered on a friend's disappointment.
Seeing it as a road trip,
the real stories of a life,
and an attempt to be a real boy.

War of 1812

The picture of the first King
    must be broken.

God has set forth a schedule,
    as the President paints
    the countryside.
    For if the fires burn
longer than two suns can turn,
    the winds shall bring
    the tears of God
and the tornado shall put out
    the fire of the British.

She's Late Again

She's late again,
reruns are raging
the gangster flick is reaching its climax
　and thoughts are jumping rope.

She's late again,
the demons
come back
　　to draw another crooked line
next to the other.

The past inefficiencies bewilder
　　　　the passing of time
in years
　　meaning experience is only
　　　　Gods will for you.

The Track They Walk

They claim to be good mothers,
but the track they walk
 is laid out on their arms,
 like the mark of the beast.
Prominent and boastful
they're homeless.
Tattooed are the numbers
of the thief,
 liar,
 and the whore.
They have done deeds
which kings in tents
 resting in the desert
 beneath the wondrous star
 have spoken against and
 words have been passed
 on for two thousand years.

Fire

Spit at me
with hells fire you
blasphemer and fornicator
you bitch.
Declare yourself unto thee,
betrayed but loved
the people wait for you
to witness the growing
because the time has come,
carbon is here,
    you must strike.

Exorcism

The thoughts transfer
in tongues,
lips are chapped
with pure
spring water.
The Pope's dream team
not available
at this time.
There are places for the poor
to pray
and state their name.
The king's horses will be
tied up out front
the king's men
will come
when Satan
has taunted them.

Monkey Information

It's as if one monkey
whispered to another
down, down the row
 they go.
Changing direction until
 a decision is made.
 Down, down fall the bodies
 from the interpretation.
 A species who can't remember
 where it came from
 brings death to
  its own clan.

The Code

We see the cross
chastise our body
and feel the temptation
of sacrifice
each living second
the church cries.
The blood of Christ
is taken whole
with the body
from his soul.
Hoping and praying
that the sins
of creators have not
damned us to drown
in the wine for which
we create our children.

The Hitchhiker

It's dark and I'm tired,
dazed with flickering lights.
I see the flowing robe
in the middle of the road.
With a thumb out for a ride,
slow to see the car pull over.
My sister who has been gone
picks up the robe and
goes the other way.
With hands he gives direction,
she pays no attention, and
takes him far away. That is
why the black cat which ran into
the street, turned around with fear
when hit by the light.

Books

In a sleep
hurt by the actions of self,
the devil is a ball and chain
showing himself within
the blood of Christ.
Ingested with certainty
is a death wish.

But then a light
comes as forgiveness,
 and the son speaks though tears,
and the crying child
allows peace to continue
with a joy
and a fondness for books.

Iran

Please don't take my little boy,
his hands have never seen powder.
Rubber bands at his brother,
and laughter was war.
His face speckled like the dunes,
faithful like the desert wonderers.
He would be too good at it,
or die trying.
His heritage would not let
him give or surrender.
For he took the land,
for which he breaths.
Please do not take my little boy,
because if asked he would go.

Grail

I am a ghost
lying witness
to my stumbling.
Befallen, murdered
by the guns
of my own nature.
I have control
and see others
as facts that dwindle
the guards of God,
light chose a foe
the holder of the Grail.
I declare,
I will return
like another
five hundred
years from now.

Junk Yard

There is life in there
underneath the mangled,
torn, and shredded carcasses
deposited one on top the other.
Forensic scientists would have a day
in the field overgrown
under-nourished with a
collection of debris
tossed away in typical
fashion of Capitalism.
What crimes are buried?
Gone unreported, sitting
waiting to be uncovered
wanting peace to be bought.
For decades it sits
until the same system
which put it there
finds more money
in planting seeds
and families there.

Place

The drinks are served
the movie is
The Wizard of Oz.
Don't look for
the witch outside.
The door is down
they feel God's will
be done.
Who shall prevail?
The plane is
the object, and
with hands
it shall crash.
Who will go
   to what place?

Strings

By the strings we
are the Roman Empire.
Paying for the leaders
concubines dressed
in nowhere.
Consumers paying
for music
written
by the hand
of a man
proclaimed by birth
to follow history
and be dads
little man standing
where Jesus
walked
asking for help.

Regrets

I've always loved your
words of
drunken slumber.
You turn life open
to the outside.
With leaves falling
from the trees.
Falling, branches
snapped and broken,
wanting to be back.
Spring is a long way,
and it always
 brings regret.

The Bible

The Bible sits
 unread
 wondering for
 a better understanding
 of children
 who will read it.
 Read it,
 ask the questions.
 Who will be there?
 Wait and see
  the regret will show you
  the time you have
  to find the answer.

Suicide at Ground Zero

I wanted to depart
yesterday
but I thought
maybe I should
just fly across
the country, and
kill someone else.

But would this act
make my feet lighter
head clearer
allow me to
take fewer steps, thus
my life could catch up?

Reaching a point now,
down hill I walk
everyday getting closer
to freezing
in the darkness.

Thanksgiving

Walking with the darkness of rain
I am pushed by the year passed
and held in pain by the earth;
in which she lay.

The ramblings and cracklings are
the price of this miscarriage
for I should have stood with all
and gave thanks that day.

Instead I cried for the future
of my own children fine
and now my life sits angry
between the walls of it's crest.

Hoping to see a youthful dawn;
I place a flower upright
and a necklace of spirituality.

www.ingramcontent.com/pod-product-compliance
Lightning Source LLC
Chambersburg PA
CBHW032135090426
42743CB00007B/608